41-53

THE SMOKELESS FIRE

The Smokeless Fire

HINDU MYSTICAL REFLECTIONS

edited and with photographs by
CATHARINE HUGHES

A CROSSROAD BOOK
THE SEABURY PRESS • **NEW YORK**

ACKNOWLEDGMENTS

The Bhagavad Gita: A New Verse Translation, by Ann Stanford. Copyright © 1970 by Herder and Herder, Inc. Reprinted by permission of the publisher.
The Life Divine, by Sri Aurobindo. Copyright 1949 by the Sri Aurobindo Library, Inc.
The Sacred Books of the East, vol. 8, translated by Kashinath Trimbak Telang. Charles Scribner's Sons, 1900.
The Thirteen Principal Upanishads, translated from the Sanskrit by Robert Ernest Hume. Oxford University Press, 1921. Reprinted by permission of the publisher.
The Upanishads: Breath of the Eternal, translated by Swami Prabhavananda and Frederick Manchester. Copyright © 1957 by the Vedanta Society of Southern California.

Designed by Joseph Vesely

Copyright © 1974 by the Seabury Press, Inc.

ISBN: 0-8164-2102-1

Manufactured in the United States of America

The wisdom and mysticism of the East have very much to give us even though they speak their own language which it is impossible to imitate. They should remind us of that which is familiar in our own culture and which we have already forgotten, and we should direct our attention to that which we have put aside as insignificant, namely the fate of our own inner man.

—Carl G. Jung

INTRODUCTION

Hinduism is generally regarded as the world's oldest faith. For many, it is not simply a religion, but plays a virtually all-pervasive role in life. It numbers well in excess of three hundred million adherents in India (eighty-five per cent of the population) and between fifteen and twenty million in other parts of Asia, the West Indies, and South Africa.

In contrast with Christianity, Buddhism, or Islam, Hinduism had no single founder. Rather, it traces its sources to the Vedas, a body of ancient and unattributed "revealed scriptures" which originated in the even more ancient hymns of the Aryan nomads who came to India in the same period that Moses was leading the people of Israel out of Egypt.

The *shruti* ("that which was heard") Vedas are the most ancient in Hinduism. Somewhat later, came the *smriti* ("that which was remembered"). The Rig Veda, written in Sanskrit and considered the most ancient Hindu text, contains this greeting to the morning sun, which many Hindus still employ today:

INTRODUCTION

Let us meditate upon the adorable
Glory of the Divine Life-Giver
And may he direct our thoughts.

The Aryans ("nobles") came into northern
India through the Himalayan passes in what
is believed to have been between 1500 and
1000 B.C., conquering the vast agricultural
civilizations of the river basins and bringing
with them their bardic priests, who were said
to possess teachings from "the very breath of
God." Their sky-gods in time merged with the
earth-fertility gods of the civilization they con-
quered, giving rise to the traditions and rituals
recorded in the Vedas. Many historians be-
lieve that the rigid Indian caste system, with
its structured social classes, is at least partially
the result of the fact that the Aryans were so
outnumbered by the native population that
they attempted to preserve their identity and
position through a stabilized and hereditary
conquerer-subject relationship.

The Vedic period came to an end by the
first millennium B.C., and the Upanishads,
apparently the work of anonymous forest
seers and among the world's oldest records
of mysticism, appeared. To this day, they re-

main for many the ultimate source of spiritual life. The Mandukya Upanishad describes the mystical consciousness as

> beyond the senses, beyond the understanding, beyond all expression. . . . It is the pure unitary consciousness, wherein awareness of the world and of multiplicity is completely obliterated. It is ineffable peace. It is the Supreme Good. It is one without a second. It is the Self.

It is reminiscent of—or, more accurately, anticipates—the Flemish Catholic mystic Jan van Ruysbroeck (1293-1381), who speaks of the "God-seeing man" whose spirit is "undifferentiated and without distinction and therefore it feels nothing but the unity."

This idea of "undifferentiated unity" is present in virtually every description of the mystical experience, though continually reinterpreted in the light of individual creeds or dogmas. The Mandukya Upanishad asserts that it "is the Self," which may seem far more philosophically complex than it in fact is. In *The Teachings of the Mystics*, Walter T. Stace asks:

INTRODUCTION

Why is the unity now identified with the Self? The answer is plain. We started with the full self or mind of our everyday consciousness. What was it full of? It was full of the multiplicity of sensations, thoughts, desires, and the rest. . . . These disparate elements were held together in a unity, the unity of the single mind or self. . . . Now when we emptied all the multiple contents out of this unity of the self what is left, according to the Upanishad, is the unity of the self, the original unity minus its contents. And this is the self.

Beyond this came another step, the identification of this individual self with the Infinite Self, the Absolute, Brahman, which those responsible for the creation of the Upanishads considered to be the secret of salvation.

By 600 B.C., Indian philosophy clearly accepted the idea of reincarnation after death. One contributing factor in this—though hardly the only one—was the rigidity of the caste system, under which the injustices of hereditary caste, which for the masses involved poverty, illness, and servitude, led to a deepseated pessimism, a conviction that the present life was essentially sorrowful, but that one

INTRODUCTION

who could attain identification with the Brahman would not be reborn with the same degradation but instead would achieve the life of the Infinite. It is this mystic union with the Divine Reality that is Hinduism's highest aim.

The idea of a "melting away" of the individual into the Infinite, into "boundless being," is common to other cultures. ("Boundless being" is in fact Tennyson's phrase.) In the Brihadarayanka Upanishad it is stated: "The individual self, dissolved, is the Eternal. . . . Where there is consciousness of the Self, individuality is no more." It has its parallel in the Christian mystics' concept of "union with God," though the latter differs in many ways.

It is, however, the *Bhagavad Gita* ("Song of the Lord"), a dialog between Arjuna, a legendary warrior, and Krishna, Brahman in human guise, that ranks as the single most important work in Hindu sacred literature.

The date of composition is uncertain, though usually placed somewhere between the fifth and second centuries B.C. As Ann Stanford notes in her admirable new verse translation, several of its verses are restatements of ideas that appeared in the Upanishads. It warns against extreme asceticism, instead advocating a middle way, the way of moderation, and suggests in addition to the traditional courses to salvation—righteousness, asceticism, and devotion—a fourth, *karma yoga,* disciplined activity, which stresses not so much the work done in one's daily life but one's attitude toward that work.

The *Bhagavad Gita* provides a treatise on man's relationship with God and that of illusion to the Real, teaching that God alone is real. It is the *Gita,* as it is usually called, that offers particular authority for the modern Hindu's willingness not to insist upon an exclusive possession of Truth, but instead also to honor Christ or the Buddha as manifestations on earth of Divine Reality in human form. Krishna says:

In every age I come back
To deliver the holy,
To destroy the sins of the sinner,
To establish righteousness.

Krishna appears in several roles in the course of the *Bhagavad Gita.* He is a clan leader and cousin of Arjuna in the epic *Mahabharata,* an incarnation of the god Vishnu, the Brahman, and the supreme and monotheistic god. In the present, one can hear his disciples—following a pattern established by

INTRODUCTION

Chaitanya (1485-1533), chanting the repeated "Hare Krishna, Hare Krishna, Rama Hare" on the streets of New York, San Francisco, and in many other parts of the Western world. In more recent times, we find Sri Aurobindo, who was born in India in 1872, voicing mystical reflections that are remarkably close to those of the Upanishads some three thousand years before. Much of his writing is based directly upon them, yet it is not merely a repetition or reproduction in more modern form, for Aurobindo sought to adapt those ancient teachings to a modern, and Western, world vastly altered by the influence of science.

Aurobindo was educated in classics at Cambridge, where he won various awards in Latin and Greek. After fourteen years in England, he returned to India, for a period teaching English literature at Baroda College, and subsequently becoming involved in the nationalistic politics of the day. The British arrested him for sedition and accused him of participating in terrorism. Shortly after his acquittal, he gave up politics and "retired from the world" in order to devote the remainder of his life to the practice of yoga and the goals of mysticism.

Aurobindo published numerous books— brief extracts appear later in this volume—

INTRODUCTION

perhaps the most significant being *The Divine Life,* in which he describes the experience of the mystic:

> The mind when it passes the gates of the Transcendent suddenly . . . receives a sense of the unreality of the world and the sole reality of the Silence which is one of the most powerful and convincing experiences of which the human mind is capable.

Aurobindo was concerned with what he apparently viewed as two poles: Western scientific materialism and Eastern idealistic mysticism, both of which he saw tending toward extremes, but each of which also possessed the potential to act as a counterweight to the other. Indeed, he went so far as to suggest that one should "observe with respect and wonder the work that Atheism has done for the Divine and admire the service that Agnosticism has rendered in preparing the illimitable increase of knowledge.

> In our world error is continually the handmaid and pathfinder of Truth; for error is really a half-truth that stumbles because

INTRODUCTION

of its limitations; often it is Truth that wears a disguise in order to arrive unobserved near to its goal.

In *Three Ways of Ancient Wisdom,* Nancy Wilson Ross acknowledges that Hinduism possesses "seemingly contradictory aspects." (It is, for instance, on the one hand, monotheistic, with a belief in one supreme Divinity, but, on the other, demonstrates many polytheistic or animistic devotional practices.) It is, as she notes, a "metaphysical labyrinth" which, at least initially, is likely to bewilder the Westerner. There is a gallery of gods and goddesses—some of them of a nature and fantastic quality virtually incomprehensible to someone from another culture—diverse rituals, ceremonials, sects, cults, and to the "outsider" an appearance of chaos. Yet, there is also a unifying—and universal—element: a belief in Brahman, ultimate, and ultimately indescribable, Reality. For those who seek it, it offers a sufficient unifying principle, mystical and even objective, goal. For, as it is stated in the Upanishads,

Reality is One though sages call it by different names.

THE SMOKELESS FIRE

The idea of limit, of the impossible, begins to grow a little shadowy and it appears instead that whatever man constantly wills, he must in the end be able to do; for the consciousness in the race eventually finds the means. It is not in the individual that this omnipotence expresses itself, but the collective Will of mankind that works out with the individual as a means. And yet when we look more deeply, it is not any conscious Will of the collectivity, but a superconscious Might that uses the individual as a center and means, the collectivity as a condition and field. What is this but the God in man, the infinite Identity, the multitudinous Unity, the Omniscient, the Omnipotent, who having made man in His own image . . . seeks to express in them some image of the unity, omniscience, omnipotence, which are the self-conception of the Divine? "That which is immortal in mortals is a God and established inwardly as an energy working out in our divine powers." It is this vast cosmic impulse which the modern world, without quite knowing its own aim, yet serves in all its activities and labors subconsciously to fulfill.

—Sri Aurobindo

Those abiding in the midst of ignorance,
Self-wise, thinking themselves learned,
Running hither and thither, go around
deluded,
Like blind men led by one who is himself
blind.

—Katha Upanishad

Fearless and pure in heart
Constant in the way of knowledge
Generous, self-controlled, reverent
Reading the holy word, austere, upright

Doing no harm, truthful, without anger
Willing to lose, at peace, not speaking ill,
With sympathy for creatures, free of greed
Gentle, modest, without wavering

Vigorous, patient, enduring, pure
Without malice and not over-proud—
Son of Bharata, such is the man
Who is born for a god-like place.

—Bhagavad Gita

One must raise the self by the self
And not let the self sink down
For the self's only friend is the self
And the self is the self's one enemy.

To the man whose self is self-subdued
His own self is a friend
But in him who does not own the self
Hostile the self abides, like a foe.

Of one who has come to rest, self-conquered,
The supreme self is calm and at peace
In cold and heat, ease and pain
In disgrace and honor.

—Bhagavad Gita

When are liberated all
The desires that lodge in
    one's heart,
Then a mortal becomes immortal!

When are cut all
The knots of the heart here
    on earth,
Then a mortal becomes immortal!
        —Katha Upanishad

He who is able here in this world
Before giving up the body
To resist the thrust of wrath and desire
He is controlled, and a happy man.

He who finds his joy within
Within, his grove of pleasure
And the light of the sun within,
Merging with God, he gains God's bliss.
                              —*Bhagavad Gita*

He who tries to give an idea of God by mere book learning is like the man who tries to give an idea of the city of Benares by means of a map or a picture.

—Sri Ramakrishna

By whom impelled soars forth the mind
    projected?
By whom enjoined goes forth the earliest
    breathing?
By whom impelled this speech do people
    utter?
The eye, the ear—what god, pray
    them enjoineth?

That which is the hearing of the ear, the
    thought of the mind,
The voice of speech, as also the breathing
    of the breath,
And the sight of the eye! Past these
    escaping, the wise,
On departing from this world, become
    immortal.
    There the eye goes not;
    Speech goes not, nor the mind.
    We know not, we understand not
    How one would teach it.
    Other, indeed, is It than the known,
    And moreover above the unknown.
    —Thus have we heard of the ancients
    Who to us have explained It.
             —Kena Upanishad

Closing up all the gates
And locking his thought in the
    heart
Placing his vital breath in the head,
Staying, supported by discipline

Saying *Om*, in one syllable
The divine secret,
    remembering me
As he leaves his body and departs
He goes to the far off goal.

Partha, I am easy to gain
For the always controlled
Who meditates on me constantly
His thoughts never going
    elsewhere.

Having come to me, great-
    souled men
Do not go back to birth,
The home of pain and the
    inconstant.
They have gone to perfection
    beyond.
            —Bhagavad Gita

The Self, which is free from evil, ageless, deathless, sorrowless, hungerless, thirstless, whose desire is the Real, whose conception is the Real—He should be searched out, Him one should desire to understand. He obtains all worlds and all desires who has found out and who understands that Self.

—Chandogya Upanishad

The touch of Earth is always reinvigorating to the son of Earth, even when he seeks a supraphysical Knowledge. It may even be said that the supraphysical can only be really mastered in its fullness—to its heights we can always reach—when we keep our feet firmly on the physical. "Earth is His footing," says the Upanishad whenever it images the Self that manifests in the universe. And it is certainly the fact that the wider we extend and the surer we make our knowledge of the physical world, the wider and surer becomes our foundation for the high knowledge.

—Sri Aurobindo

The faith of men is of three kinds,
It springs from their own natures—
Good, passionate, or dull.
Hear how it is.

The faith of every man
Is in tune with his true being
A man is made of his faith
What his faith is, so is he.

Men of goodness worship the shining gods,
Men of passion, gods of wealth and power.
The others, the people of darkness
Worship ghosts and crowds of spirits.
                    —*Bhagavad Gita*

He who has devoted his self to abstraction,
by devotion looking alike on everything,
sees the self abiding in all beings,
and all beings in the self.
To him who sees me in everything,
and everything in me,
I am never lost
and he is not lost to me.
The worshipper who worships me
abiding in all beings,
holding that all is one,
lives in me
however he may be living.

—*Bhagavad Gita*

Him who is without beginning and without
    end, in the midst of confusion,
The creator of all, of manifold form,
The One embracer of the universe—
By knowing God one is released from
    all fetters.

Him who is to be apprehended in existence,
    who is called "incorporeal,"
The maker of existence and non-existence,
    the kindly one,
God, the maker of the creation and
    its parts—
They who know Him, have left the body
    behind.

—Svetasvatara Upanishad

Speech is not what one should desire to understand. One should know the speaker.

Smell is not what one should desire to understand. One should know the smeller.

Form is not what one should desire to understand. One should know the seer.

Sound is not what one should desire to understand. One should know the hearer.

Taste is not what one should desire to understand. One should know the discerner of taste.

The deed is not what one should desire to understand. One should know the doer.

Pleasure and pain are not what one should desire to understand. One should know the discerner of pleasure and pain.

Bliss, delight, and procreation are not what one should desire to understand. One should know the discerner of bliss, delight, and procreation.

Going is not what one should desire to understand. One should know the goer.

Mind is not what one should desire to understand. One should know the thinker.

—Kaushitaki Upanishad

The ancient narrow path that stretches
    far away
Has been touched by me, has been found
    by me.
By it the wise, the knowers of Brahma, go up
Hence to the heavenly world, released.
              —Brihadaranyaka Upanishad

In emerging out of the materialistic period of human Knowledge we must be careful that we do not rashly condemn what we are leaving or throw away even one tittle of its gains, before we can summon perceptions and powers that are well grasped and secure, to occupy their place.

—Sri Aurobindo

The separate nature of the senses,
And that their arising and setting
Is of things that come into being apart
　　[from himself],
The wise man recognizes, and sorrows not.

Higher than the senses is the mind;
Above the mind is the true being.
Over the true being is the Great Self
　　[intellect];
Above the Great is the Unmanifest.

Higher than the Unmanifest, however, is
　　the Person,
All-pervading and without any mark
　　whatever.
Knowing which, a man is liberated
And goes to immortality.

His form is not to be beheld.
No one soever sees Him with the eye.
He is framed by the heart, by the thought,
　　by the mind.
They who know That become immortal.
　　　　　　　　—Katha Upanishad

Know thou the soul as riding in a chariot,
The body as the chariot.
Know thou the intellect as the
    chariot-driver,
And the mind as the reins.

The senses, they say, are the horses;
The objects of sense, what they range over.
The self combined with senses and mind
Wise men call "the enjoyer."

He who has not understanding,
Whose mind is not constantly held firm—
His senses are uncontrolled,
Like the vicious horses of a chariot-driver.

He, however, who has understanding,
Whose mind is constantly held firm—
His senses are under control,
Like the good horses of a chariot-driver.
                    —Katha Upanishad

In our world error is continually the handmaid and pathfinder of Truth; for error is really a half-truth that wears a disguise in order to arrive unobserved near to its goal.
—Sri Aurobindo

Devoted to his own proper work
A man gains fulfillment.
How, rejoicing in his work
He reaches this perfection,
    now hear.

By honoring with his own work
Him from whom beings came
Who stretched forth all this
    universe
A man reaches perfection.

Better his own duty, imperfect,
Than another's task well done.
He brings on himself no stain
Who works in accord with his
    nature.
            —*Bhagavad Gita*

Of this great tree, if someone should strike at the root, it would bleed, but still live. If someone should strike at its middle, it would bleed, but still live. If someone should strike at its top, it would bleed, but still live. Being pervaded by Atman [Soul], it continues to stand, eagerly drinking in moisture and rejoicing.

If the life leaves one branch of it, then it dries up. It leaves a second; then that dries up. It leaves a third; then that dries up. It leaves the whole; the whole dries up. . . .

When life has left it, this body dies. The life does not die. That which is the finest essence—this whole world has that as its soul. That is Reality. That is Atman [Soul].

—Chandogya Upanishad

In every age I come back
To deliver the holy,
To destroy the sins of the sinner,
To establish righteousness.
—*Bhagavad Gita*

Arise ye! Awake ye!
Obtain your boons [answers] and understand
    them!
A sharpened edge of a razor, hard to
    traverse,
A difficult path is this—poets declare!

What is soundless, touchless, formless,
    imperishable,
Likewise tasteless, constant, odorless,
Without beginning, without end, higher than
    the great, stable—
By discerning That, one is liberated from the
    mouth of death.
                  —Katha Upanishad

According as one acts, according as one conducts himself, so does he become. The doer of good becomes good. The doer of evil becomes evil. One becomes virtuous by virtuous action, bad by bad action.

—Brihadaranyaka Upanishad

Truth alone conquers, not falsehood.
By truth is laid out the path leading
    to the gods
By which the sages whose desire
    is satisfied ascend
To where is the highest repository
    of truth.
                    —Mundaka Upanishad

Matter is perishable. The Lord, the destroyer of ignorance, is imperishable, immortal. He is the one God, the Lord of the perishable and of all souls. By meditating on him, by uniting oneself with him, by identifying oneself with him, one ceases to be ignorant.

—Svetasvatara Upanishad

Each acts in accord with his own nature,
Even the man who is wise.
Creatures follow nature.
What can coercion do?

Every sense has objects
That cause loathing or love—
You must not fall under their rule
Though the two stalk your path.

Better do your own task imperfectly
Than do another's well.
Better die in your own duty
Another's task brings peril.

—*Bhagavad Gita*

Truth is what *is*—and that is the beauty of it.

—Sri Krishnamurti

Those who with the eye of wisdom
See the difference between
    field and knower
And how beings are freed out
    of nature
They go to the beyond.
            —Bhagavad Gita

The truth is that you are always united with the Lord. But you must *know* this. Nothing further is there to know. Meditate, and you will realize that mind, matter, and Maya [the power which unites mind and matter] are but three aspects of Brahman, the one reality.

Fire, though present in the firesticks, is not perceived until one stick is rubbed against another. The Self is like that fire: it is realized in the body by meditation of the sacred syllable OM. . . .

Like oil in sesame seeds, butter in cream, water in the river bed, fire in tinder, the Self dwells within the soul. Realize him through truthfulness and meditation.

Like butter in cream is the Self in everything. Knowledge of the Self is gained through meditation. The Self is Brahman. By Brahman is all ignorance destroyed.

—Svetasvatara Upanishad

When one gives without hope
    of return
To a worthy man at the right place
    and time
Thinking only *one must give*
That gift is of goodness.

But when one gives for a return
Or has a special aim in view
Or is deeply troubled by giving
His gift is deemed to be of passion.

And given at the wrong place
    and time
To the wrong person
Not with kindness but with contempt
That gift is given in darkness.
                 —Bhagavad Gita

If, with love, one stretches out to me
A leaf, a blossom, fruit, or water
I take from that devoted soul
The heart-given offering.

Whatever you do, whatever you eat
Whatever you give, whatever you offer
Whatever austerities you undergo,
. . . . . . do as an offering to me.

Thus you will be released
From the bonds of action, its fair and
     evil fruits,
Your self trained in the discipline of denial.
Freed, you will move swiftly to me.

I am the same in all beings
No one is hateful or dear to me
But those who turn to me with love
Are in me, and I too am in them.
               —*Bhagavad Gita*

One looks upon It as a wonder,
another speaks of It as a wonder,
another hears of It as a wonder,
and even after having heard of It,
no one really does know It.

—*Bhagavad Gita*

What is the cause of this universe? Whence do we come? Why do we live? Where shall we at last find rest? Under whose command are we bound by the law of happiness and its opposite?

Time, space, law, chance, matter, primal energy, intelligence—none of these, nor a combination of these, can be the final cause of the universe, for they are effects, and exist to serve the soul. Nor can the individual self be the cause, for being subject to the law of happiness and misery, it is not free.

—Svetasvatara Upanishad

Laying down works done out of desire
The wise call renouncing.
Giving up all results of action
The seers call abandonment.

Some wise men say action is tainted
It should be abandoned.
Others say sacrifice, giving, and penance
Are works that should not be given up.

* * * * * *

Works of sacrifice, giving, and penance
Should not be set aside, but done.
Through sacrifice, austerities, giving
Men who understand are made pure.

* * * * * *

To renounce a work that should be done
Is not fitting.
To cast it aside through illusion
Is said to stem from darkness.

When a man cries *It is too hard!*
And for fear of bodily toil
Gives up work, he does it from passion.
He earns nothing by such renouncing.

But if he says *This work must be done!*
And does whatever is required
Giving up desire and reward
His abandonment comes from goodness.
                              —*Bhagavad Gita*

The wise, full of love, worship me
believing that I am the origin of all
and that all moves on through me.
Placing their minds on me,
offering their lives to me,
instructing each other and speaking about me
they are always contented and happy.
To these who are constantly devoted
and who worship with love
I give that knowledge by which they
        attain to me.
And remaining in their hearts,
I destroy with the brilliant lamp of knowledge
the darkness born of ignorance in
        such men only
out of compassion for them.
                    —*Bhagavad Gita*

The Self . . . is to be known. Hear about it, reflect upon it, meditate upon it. By knowing the Self, my beloved, through hearing, reflection, and meditation, one comes to know all things. . . . The priest, the warrior, the higher worlds, the gods, the creatures, whatsoever things there be—these are the Self.

—Brihadaranyaka Upanishad

Two birds, fast bound companions,
Clasp close the self-same tree.
Of these two, the one eats sweet fruit;
The other looks on without eating.

On the self-same tree a person, sunken,
Grieves for his impotence, deluded;
When he sees the other, the Lord, contented,
And his greatness, he becomes freed
    from sorrow.

When a seer sees the brilliant
Maker, Lord, Person, the Brahma-source,
Then, being a knower, shaking off good
    and evil,
Stainless, he attains supreme identity
    [with Him].
                —Mundaka Upanishad

Even as a mirror stained by dust
Shines brilliantly when it has
 been cleansed,
So the embodied one, on seeing
 the nature of the Soul
Becomes unitary, his end attained,
 from sorrow freed.

When with the nature of the self,
 as with a lamp,
A practiser of Yoga beholds here
 the nature of Brahma,
Unborn, steadfast, from every
 nature free—
By knowing God one is released
 from all fetters!
   —Svetasvatara Upanishad

Vast, heavenly, of unthinkable form,
And more minute than the minute, It
    shines forth.
It is farther than the far, yet here
    near at hand,
Set down in the secret place [of the heart],
    even here among those who behold [It].

Not by sight is It grasped, not
    even by speech,
Not by any other sense-organs, austerity,
    or work.
By the peace of knowledge, one's
    nature purified—
In that way, however, by meditating, one
    does behold Him who is without parts.
          —Mundaka Upanishad

Whatever is here, that is there.
What is there, that again is here.
He obtains death after death
Who seems to see a difference here.

By the mind, indeed, is this [realization]
    to be attained—
There is no difference here at all!
He goes from death to death
Who seems to see a difference here.
                   —Katha Upanishad

In the beginning this world was Brahma, the limitless One—limitless to the east, limitless to the south, limitless to the west, limitless to the north, and above and below, limitless in every direction. Truly, for him east and the other directions exist not, nor across, nor below, nor above.

Incomprehensible is that supreme Soul, unlimited, unborn, not to be reasoned about, unthinkable—He whose soul is space! In the dissolution of the world He alone remains awake. From that space He, assuredly, awakes this world, which is a mass of thought. It is thought by Him, and in Him it disappears.

His is that shining form which gives heat in yonder sun and which is the brilliant light in a smokeless fire, as also the fire in the stomach which cooks food. For thus has it been said: "He who is in the fire, and he who is here in the heart, and he who is yonder in the sun—he is one."

—Maitri Upanishad

The better is one thing, and the
    pleasanter quite another.
Both these, of different aim,
    bind a person.
Of these two, well is it for him
    who takes the better;
He fails of his aim who chooses
    the pleasanter.

Both the better and the pleasanter
    come to a man.
Going all around the two, the wise
    · man discriminates.
The wise man chooses the better,
    indeed, rather than the
        pleasanter.
The stupid man, from getting-and-
    keeping, chooses the
        pleasanter.
                —Katha Upanishad

It is necessary that advancing Knowledge should base herself on a clear, pure, and disciplined intellect. It is necessary, too, that she should correct her errors sometimes by a return to the restraint of sensible fact, the concrete realities of the physical world.

—Sri Aurobindo

People say: "A person is made [not of acts, but] of desires only." [In reply to this I say:] As is his desire, such is his resolve; as is his resolve, such the action he performs; what action he performs, that he procures for himself [into that does he become changed].
—Brihadaranyaka Upanishad

Know God, and all fetters will be loosed. Ignorance will vanish. Birth, death, and rebirth will be no more. Meditate upon him and transcend physical consciousness. Thus will you reach union with the lord of the universe. Thus will you become identified with him who is One without a second. In him all your desires will find fulfillment.

—Svetasvatara Upanishad

The childish go after outward
        pleasures;
They walk into the net of
        widespread death.
But the wise, knowing immortality,
Seek not the stable among things
        which are unstable here.
                    —Katha Upanishad

Not by speech, not by mind,
Not by sight can He be apprehended.
How can He be comprehended
Otherwise than by one's saying "He is"?

He can indeed be comprehended by the
       thought "He is"
And by [admitting] the real nature of both
       [his comprehensibility and his
           incomprehensibility].
When he has been comprehended by the
       thought "He is"
His real nature manifests itself.
                              —Katha Upanishad

The seer sees not death,
Nor sickness, nor any distress.
The seer sees only the All,
Obtains the All entirely.
                    —Maitri Upanishad

He who knows Brahman,
whose mind is steady,
who is not deluded,
and who rests in Brahman,
does not exult on finding
    anything agreeable
nor does he grieve on finding
    anything disagreeable.
One whose self is not attached to
    external objects,
obtains the happiness that is
    in the self,
and through concentration of mind,
joining one's self with the Brahman,
one obtains indestructible
    happiness . . .
The worshipper whose happiness
    is within,
whose recreation is within
and whose light also is within,
obtains divine bliss
becoming one with the Brahman . . .
He attains tranquility,
knowing me to be the enjoyer
of all sacrifices and penances,
the Great Lord of all worlds
and the friend of all beings.
                  —*Bhagavad Gita*

When a person departs from this world he goes to the wind. It opens out there for him like the hole of a chariot-wheel. Through it he mounts higher.

He goes to the sun. It opens out there for him like the hole of a drum. Through it he mounts higher.

He goes to the moon. It opens out for him there like the hole of a kettle-drum. Through it he mounts higher.

He goes to the world that is without heat, without cold. Therein he dwells eternal years.

—Brihadaranyaka Upanishad

As a heavily loaded cart goes creaking, just so this bodily self, mounted by the intelligent Self, goes groaning when one is breathing one's last.

When he comes to weakness—whether he come to weakness through old age or through disease—this person frees himself from these limbs just as a mango, or a fig, or a berry releases itself from its bond; and he hastens again, according to the entrance and place of origin, back to life.

—Brihadaranyaka Upanishad

They who practice austerity and
     faith in the forest,
The peaceful knowers who live
     on alms,
Depart passionless through the
     door of the sun,
To where is that immortal Person,
     e'en the imperishable Spirit.
          —Mundaka Upanishad

Into blind darkness enter they
That worship ignorance;
Into darkness greater than that,
    as it were, they
That delight in knowledge.

Other, indeed, they say, than knowledge!
Other, they say, than non-knowledge!
—Thus we have heard from the wise
Who to us have explained It.

Knowledge and non-knowledge—
He who this pair conjointly knows,
With non-knowledge passing over death,
With knowledge wins the immortal.
              —Isa Upanishad

The source of the net of delusion is the fact of the association of one who is worthy of heaven with those who are not worthy of heaven. That is it. Although a grove is said to be before them, they cling to a low shrub.

By the jugglery of a doctrine that denies
    the Soul,
By false comparisons and proofs
Disturbed, the world does not discern
What is the difference between
    knowledge and ignorance.
                —Maitri Upanishad

From the unreal lead me to the real.
From darkness lead me to light.
From death lead me to immortality.
—Brihadaranyaka Upanishad

Into blind darkness enter they
That worship ignorance;
Into darkness greater than that,
    as it were, they
That delight in knowledge.

Joyless are those worlds called,
Covered with blind darkness.
To them after death go those
People that have not knowledge,
    that are not awakened.

If a person knew the Soul
With the thought "I am he!"
With what desire, for love of what
Would he cling unto the body?
    —Brihadaranyaka Upanishad

The Inner Soul of all things,
    the One Controller,
Who makes his one form manifold—
The wise who perceive Him as standing
    in oneself,
They, and no others, have eternal happiness!

Him who is the Constant among the
    inconstant, the Intelligent among
        intelligences,
The One among many, who grants desires—
The wise who perceive Him as
    standing in oneself,
They, and no others, have eternal peace!
                        —Katha Upanishad

As a tree of the forest,
Just so, surely, is man.
His hairs are leaves,
His skin the outer bark.

From his skin blood,
Sap from the bark flows forth.
From him when pierced there
        comes forth
A stream, as from the tree
        when struck.

            *   *   *   *   *   *

A tree, when it is felled, grows up
From the root, more new again;
A mortal, when cut down by death—
From what root does he grow up?

Say not "from semen,"
For that is produced from the living,
As the tree, forsooth, springing
        from seed,
Clearly arises without having died.

If with its roots they should pull up
The tree, it would not come into
        being again.
A mortal, when cut down by death—
From what root does he grow up?

When born, indeed, he is not
        born [again].
Who would again beget him?
            —Brihadaranyaka Upanishad

The sun shines not there, nor the
    moon and stars,
These lightnings shine not, much
    less this [earthly] fire!
After Him, as He shines, doth
    everything shine,
This whole world is illumined
    with His light.
                    —Katha Upanishad

I think not "I know well";
Yet I know not "I know not"!
He of us who knows It, knows It;
Yet he knows not "I know not."

It is conceived of by him by whom
    It is not conceived of.
He by whom It is conceived of,
    knows It not.
It is not understood by those who
    [say they] understand It.
It is understood by those who
    [say they] understand It not.
                —Kena Upanishad

When are liberated all
The desires that lodge in one's heart,
Then a mortal becomes immortal!
            —Brihadaranyaka Upanishad

92915